Silver

Throughout history, people of every race and culture have treasured the pure-white shine of silver, the "mother of metals." Attracted by both its beauty and its value, people have has always longed to possess it, wear it, and spend it in the form of silver coins. In the past, silver was used mainly for jewelry, decoration and money, but now silver is not only one of the world's rarest and most beautiful metals, it is also one of the most useful. Because of its special properties, it plays an important part in industry, photography, medicine and even space exploration. This book looks at the mining and refining of silver, and shows the many uses, traditional and modern, to which it is put. The author, Graham Rickard, is a professional writer, and has produced many books for children on a wide range of subjects.

Spotlight on
SILVER

Graham Rickard

ROURKE ENTERPRISES INC.
Vero Beach, Florida 32964

Cover *Silver coins of the Austro-Hungarian Empire.*

Text © 1988 Rourke Enterprises Inc.
PO Box 3328, Vero Beach, Florida 32964

Printed in Italy by G. Canale & C.S.p.A., Turin

Library of Congress Cataloging-in-Publication Data

Rickard, Graham.
    Spotlight on silver/Graham Rickard.
        p.   cm. – (Spotlight on resources)
    Bibliography: p.
    Includes index.
    Summary: Discusses the mining of silver and its processing into
objects with technological, medicinal, industrial, and artistic
uses.
    ISBN 0–86592–273–X
    1. Silver – Juvenile literature.   [1. Silver.]   I. Title.
II. Title: Silver.   III. Series.
TN761.6.R52   1988
669′.23 – dc19   87–35059
                                                         CIP
                                                          AC

Contents

1. What is silver?

Silver, like gold and platinum, is considered a precious metal because of its rarity and price. Although it is found in many countries throughout the world, the total amount of silver in the earth's crust is small compared with other metals. That is why it costs about fifty times more than copper, and 500 times more than iron. But it is the cheapest of the precious metals, costing about a twentieth the price of gold, and only one-fiftieth the price of platinum, because both these metals are even rarer than silver.

The secret of silver's beauty lies in its pure-

A vein of silver shows clearly in this nugget.

white shine. It is, in fact, the whitest of all metals, and one of the most reflective. When properly polished, it reflects about 95 percent of the light hitting its surface.

Unlike most metals, silver does not combine easily with natural chemicals; because it does not rust or corrode, its beauty is everlasting. Silver ornaments, ceremonial vessels and decorations have been found in perfect condition in the royal tombs of Egypt, dating back to 4000 B.C., and many families have silver heirlooms that have been passed from generation to generation for centuries. Some of the gases that pollute the atmosphere, such as hydrogen sulfide, do cause a dark gray film on the surface of the metal, but this tarnish is easily removed with polish.

Silver is both very malleable and ductile, so a craftsman can easily beat it into a thin layer or shape, or draw it out into a fine wire. Because it is a soft metal, like gold, finished articles can be decorated by engraving or stamping the surface with a pattern or design.

Silver is the world's best conductor of heat and electricity, and is used as a standard to measure the conductivity of all other metals. It also kills germs by absorbing the oxygen that they need to survive. Some silver salts and compounds are sensitive to light. It is this unique range of special properties that makes silver play such an important part in our world.

Right *A set of silver casters, made in England during the seventeenth century, still as bright as on the day they were made.*

7

2. The history of silver

Silver, together with gold and copper, was one of the first metals to be discovered when the human race was beginning to emerge from the Stone Age. The oldest surviving silver objects are about 6,000 years old, and the Pharaohs of ancient Egypt valued silver even more than gold, because it was more difficult to mine and extract. In the following centuries, the art of silversmithing spread around the Mediterranean countries and into northern Europe.

The vast Roman Empire included many silver-mining areas, and the Romans built large factories to produce silver for ornaments, decoration and beautiful tableware. Their method of producing

The mint at Potosi, in South America, with the stamps from which Spanish coins were made.

Above *A sixteenth-century map of Potosi, showing the Cerro Rico (rich hill).*

were soon exhausted, and the European mints desperately needed a new source. The problem was solved in the sixteenth century, when Spanish explorers discovered vast silver deposits in Central and South America. For centuries, the Aztec Indians of Mexico and the Incas of Peru had mined and worked silver, filling vast treasure houses with priceless and beautiful treasures. But the Spaniards were interested in wealth, not art, and the treasures were all melted down into ingots and shipped back to Spain in enormous quantities. In Bolivia, in 1545, they also discovered the great silver mine of Potosi, high in the mountains. Forcing local Indians to work as slave labor, the proceeds of this mine ended up as Spanish coins. That was the age of pirates, who sailed the seas in fast ships, flying the Jolly Roger, searching for Spanish treasure galleons to attack and plunder.

Below *A silver alpaca, one of the treasures of the Inca civilization.*

silver by heating the ore in a furnace continued long after the Empire had crumbled.

In the Middle Ages, there was a great increase in trade and population in European countries, and more and more silver was needed. The German mines that provided most of this silver

9

3. Where silver is found

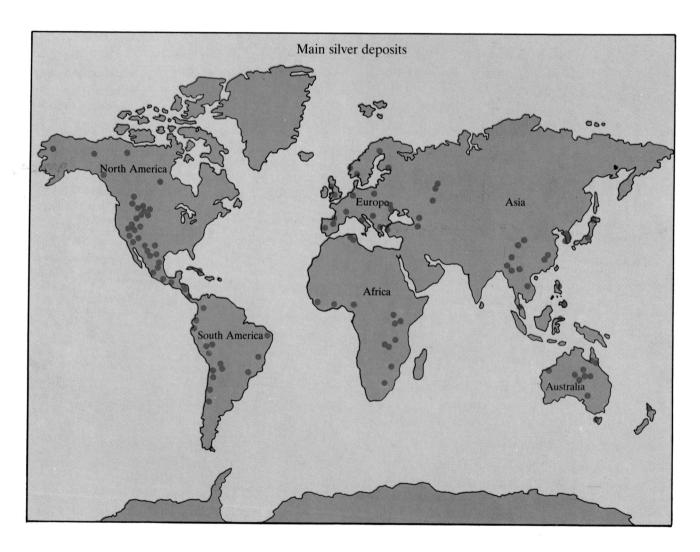

Main silver deposits

North America

South America

Europe

Asia

Africa

Australia

Map showing the areas of the world where silver is found.

Silver deposits are very widely distributed throughout all five continents of the earth, but in relatively small quantities. The search for silver has led men all over the world, but there has never been a silver rush on the same scale as the great gold rushes of the nineteenth century, because silver is rarely found in rich seams.

Like gold, silver is sometimes found in a pure, natural state, in nuggets or veins running across the surface of a rock. The largest nugget of natural silver ever found weighed 2,750 lb troy, and was discovered in Sonora, Mexico. A single mass found in Norway weighed 1,533 pounds (697 kg), but such finds are rare, and silver is usually found as a compound, such as argentite, the name given to silver sulfide. But even these compounds are found in fairly small quantities, and many tons of ore have to be mined to produce just a few ounces of silver. (Precious metals are usually sold by the troy ounce, which equals 31.1 grams.)

Unlike gold, silver is easily formed into compounds with other metals, and most silver today comes as a by-product of mining for other metals, such as lead, copper and zinc. Mining for silver alone is no longer profitable in most areas, despite efficient modern mining methods.

There are still silver mines in central Europe, which produced most of the world's silver until the discovery of the New World of the Americas. The large silver deposits at Cerro de Pasco, Peru, have been worked since the seventeenth century. In Australia, the mines at Mt. Isa and North Broken Hill are becoming large producers, while Arizona, Utah and Colorado refine silver from their copper, lead and zinc ores.

Although silver is produced all over the world, the main producers are Canada, the United States, Russia, Peru and Mexico. Among them, these countries produce more than half the world's silver supply.

Right *A copper mine in Australia where silver is also found.*

4. Mining silver

The earliest silver mines were just rough holes in the ground, dug with crude picks and shovels, made of wood, stone or antlers. As tools and techniques improved, the mine shafts became deeper, with the roofs of side passages supported on wooden pitprops and beams. The discovery of explosives for blasting the ore-bearing rock produced even deeper shafts, and mining became quicker, but more dangerous. Rock-falls, flooding, pockets of poisonous or explosive gas, and the lack of fresh air were the main hazards, as miners daily risked death to blast and hack the precious silver deposits from the ground.

Digging the tunnels in the Black Mountain silver mine in South Africa.

A mine at North Broken Hill, Australia, where silver, lead and zinc ores are found.

Modern mines have several large passages, following veins of metal ore, leading off from a large main shaft. The mine is ventilated by pumping air down from the surface, while any underground water is pumped to the surface to prevent flooding. Waste rock and ore are loaded into wagons, which usually run on rails to the main shaft, where they are hauled to the surface by the winding gear at the top of the shaft. Miners are lowered by elevator down the main shaft, which can be several miles deep, to the working face.

Modern miners use special drills and machinery to bore holes in the rock, which are filled with explosive and blasted, before clearing away the rubble and valuable ore. The machinery is a great help, but it is still back-breaking and dangerous work, in unpleasant conditions. The natural temperature of the rock in deep mines is 113°F (45°C), and the drills constantly throw out a stream of water to wash away the dust and cool the drill-bit, so the mine is usually very hot and very wet. The most dangerous part of the miners' work is the dynamite blasting. This is usually done at the end of a working shift, under very strict safety precautions.

13

5. Extracting silver from the ore

Precious metal-containing materials are melted – an early stage in the refining process.

After the ore has been brought up from the mine, it is separated from the waste rock, and several different methods are used to extract the silver, depending on the type of ore.

If the ore contains only gold and silver, it is first crushed, then treated with a solution of sodium cyanide, which dissolves both metals. When powdered zinc is added to this solution, the precious metals separate from the fluid as a sludge, which later has to be separated and refined into bars of gold and silver bullion.

With lead ore, the silver is extracted by a process called cupellation, which is mentioned in the Old Testament of the Bible, and has been used for thousands of years. The crushed ore is laid on a porous bed of bone-ash and other materials, and heated to 1,832°F (1,000°C) in a furnace with a draft of air running through it. The lead and other impurities are absorbed into the porous bed of the furnace, while the molten silver is drawn off and poured into molds to cool. A more modern method is to add zinc to the lead ore, which is then heated to the melting point of zinc, which then combines with the precious metals and separates in the form of a scum. This is strained off and then treated with the cupellation process. In this way, 98 percent of the silver present in lead ore can be extracted.

Most silver today, however, is extracted by the froth flotation process, which was discovered in 1910. With this method, the particles of crushed ore are put into a large bath, and air is passed through the ore and water mixture. The particles of metal compounds stick to the air bubbles and rise to the surface as a scum, which is smelted in a furnace and separated into the different metals. The final bars of gold or silver are still not totally pure and have to be refined before they can be sold.

Much of the silver bullion today is not mined at all, but is recovered as scrap silver from jewelers and factories, or from photographic films and chemicals.

Impurities are absorbed into the bed of the furnace, and the molten silver is poured off.

6. Extraction processes

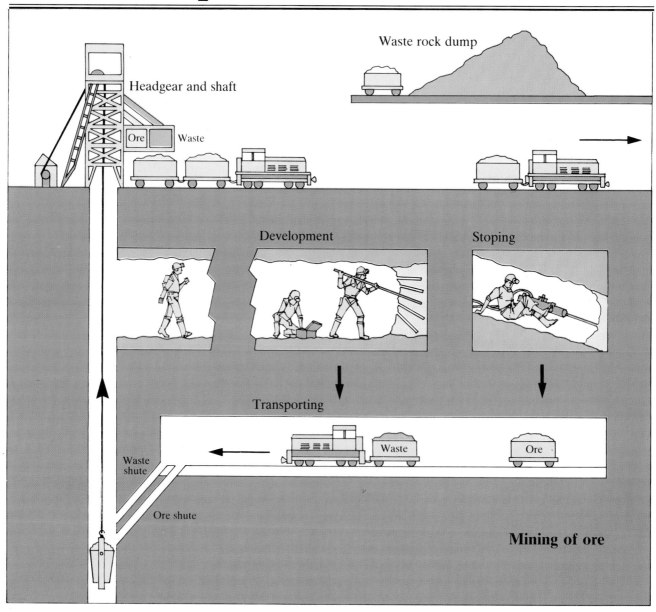

Headgear and shaft

Ore | Waste

Waste rock dump

Development

Stoping

Transporting

Waste shute

Ore shute

Waste

Ore

Mining of ore

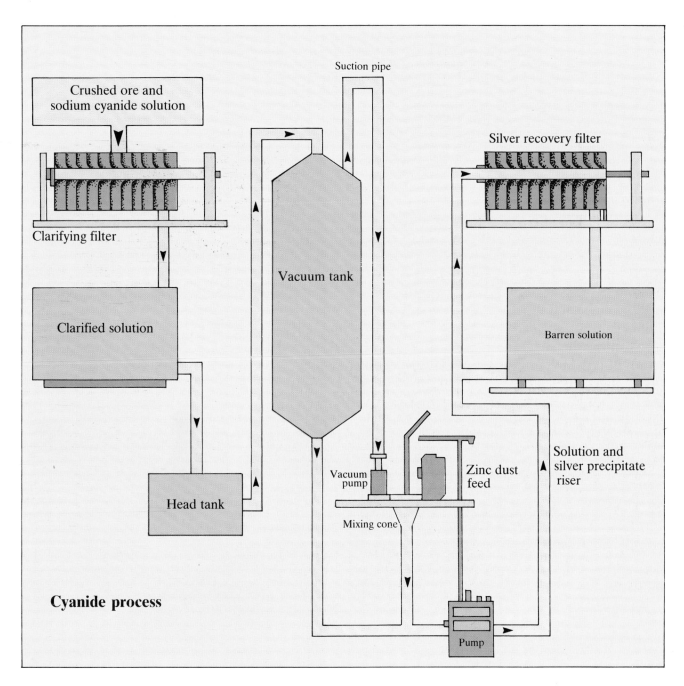

Cyanide process

17

7. Refining silver

Whichever process is used to extract the metal from the ore, silver bullion contains many impurities and has to be refined before it can be sold to jewelers or factories as pure silver.

Some bullion consists of a mixture of gold and silver, called *doré*. In the wet method of separating the two, the bullion is immersed in hot concentrated acid, either sulfuric or nitric, which dissolves the silver, leaving behind the gold. The resulting solution of silver sulfate or nitrate is treated with ferrous sulfate, which turns the silver into a sludge. This is filtered off and melted down to produce bars of silver that are 99.5 percent pure. Another method, called electrolysis, is similar to silver plating and produces even purer silver – 99.9 percent pure. In this process, the *doré* is suspended in a bath of silver nitrate solution, which also contains a sheet of pure silver or stainless steel. When an electrical current is passed through the solution between the two metals, the silver transfers itself from the *doré* (called the anode) and forms a thin sheet of pure silver on the metal sheet (which is called the cathode).

When the bullion contains a large amount of

Right *High-purity silver is removed from an electrolytic cell in the refinery.*

Pouring molten silver into molds at the Rand Refinery in South Africa.

impurities, it has to be smelted in a small furnace with lead oxide to produce a slag that can then be processed in a lead smelter. The resulting lead bullion is then melted, and the silver separated by cupellation, as described in Chapter 5.

Silver can be recovered from used photographic film by burning it and dissolving the ashes in nitric acid. This produces a solution of silver nitrate, which is then treated with sodium chloride (salt). The silver comes out as a sludge, which is filtered, melted and cast into bars. Waste silver from jeweler's workshops is also melted down to be used again.

8. The art of the silversmith

Silver is too soft to be used to make tools or weapons, but ever since its pure-white sparkle first caught their eye, people have used it to make beautiful objects of everlasting value.

Silversmithing is one of the world's oldest occupations. An ornate silver cup found in Crete dates from about 2000 B.C., and the art was well established in ancient Egypt by 1500 B.C. Many early pieces of silverware, such as candlesticks and chalices, were made for religious use, and some temples and churches had entire altars made of silver.

Pure silver is too soft even for jewelry and ornaments, so it is usually hardened by mixing it with copper to produce "sterling" or "standard" silver (containing 92.5 percent pure silver).

Silver is easy to work, and sheets of it can be bent and hammered into shape. This makes the metal brittle and liable to crack, so it has to be annealed every so often, to restore malleability. That involves heating the silver to 1,112-1,202°F (600–650°C) for about a minute, before quenching it in cold water. This makes the copper content of the metal turn black, so the metal has to be "pickled" in hot acid to

Left *A Turkish silversmith, using methods passed down through the centuries.*

Above *A silversmith beating out coins in a horn mold.*

Below *Silver mustard pots, made in the eighteenth and nineteenth centuries.*

restore the rich shine of the silver. Separate pieces are joined by heating silver solder until it melts over the joint.

Objects can easily be cast in silver by pouring hot molten metal into a mold. A silver copy is cast from a plaster mold, which is first modeled from wax. These copies are mounted into clusters in a metal flask, which is filled with plaster. When the plaster has set hard, the flask is put into a hot furnace. The wax melts and is poured away, and silver granules are put into the red-hot flask. These melt and fill the cavities left by the wax. When the flask is cool, the plaster is broken away to reveal the copies cast in silver.

Whatever method the silversmith uses, the final object can be decorated with stamped patterns or engraved designs, before being given a final polish.

9. Silver jewelry

People probably started decorating their bodies before they ever thought of wearing clothes. Throughout most of history, jewelry has been worn for ceremonial and religious occasions, as a talisman to ward off bad luck, and as a sign of social rank. Even today, people in important positions, such as kings, bishops and mayors, wear crowns, chains and rings as symbols of their power. In ancient civilizations, it was a common custom to bury the dead with their finest clothes and ornaments, and it is only in the last centuries that people have started wearing jewelry purely for personal ornament.

Jewelry can be made from anything that is considered rare and beautiful, and in the past materials have included shells, bone, pebbles and ivory. Later societies discovered enamels, gems, ceramics and precious metals, including silver. After gold, silver became the most popular metal for jewelry, because it is both beautiful and easy to work, even with primitive tools.

Apart from precious metals, the most widely used materials are gems, including such precious stones as diamonds, emeralds, rubies and sapphires. Silver is often used as a setting for transparent stones because it reflects enough light to make the stone sparkle.

In ancient times, silver ingots were beaten flat with stone hammers, and cut to size with flint knives. These shapes were then decorated by embossing a design on the front, or by hammering the reverse side of the metal sheet into a mold – a technique known as *repoussé*. Sometimes the surface was engraved with a

A gold and silver earring from an early South American civilization.

22

sharp tool, of stone or metal, called a graver. Before the technique of welding was discovered, the separate pieces had to be joined, by hammering them together, fixing them with metal pins, or binding them with silver wire.

Gem settings have a rim of silver, called a collet, which is beaten down around the stone to hold it securely in place. Otherwise powdered glass can be melted inside the rim to give an enameled finish.

Silver is a popular metal for jewelry because it is both easy to work and beautiful.

10. Modern silversmithing

The traditional craftsmanship of the silversmith still survives in many countries, but most silverware today is made by machine, using modern factory methods. These factories can produce jewelry and silver tableware much faster than handmade products, to be sold at prices that most people can afford.

Manufacturers buy their silver in bulk from the international market, usually in bars of bullion or sterling (standard) silver. Sometimes the silver is supplied already shaped for various uses, such as tubes to be cut into rings, wire for chains, granules for casting, or sheets to be stamped and cut into larger articles. Special parts such as hinges, pins and clasps, called findings, are made of a harder silver alloy and are supplied by specialist manufacturers.

Any article first has to be designed, using drawings and scale models, before the machinery is geared up for production by highly skilled staff. When each part has been made, it still has to be soldered together by hand, before being

Factories can produce modern jewelry far quicker than any silversmith.

Delicate work such as mending jewelry still has to be done by hand.

cleaned in hot acid and finally polished.

It is an extremely slow and expensive process to make silver chains by hand, and the jewelry trade uses vast amounts of these chains every year. In a modern factory, silver wire is fed into a machine that cuts, shapes and joins each link. The chains are then dipped in powdered solder and passed through a furnace on a conveyor belt, which can solder 6,000 links every hour.

Finished articles are often decorated by stamping or cutting a design into the surface, and are then highly polished. Other surface textures are now very popular. Sandblasting, for example, gives a matt finish, while different abrasive tools can be used to give a bark finish or a satin finish. Any final touches, such as setting precious stones into rings and bangles, have to done by hand.

11. Assaying and hallmarking

Most silver articles are marked with the name of the silversmith or manufacturer as well as an indication of the amount of silver they contain. To be marked sterling, an article must be 92.5 percent silver. An even higher standard is Britannia, which must be 92.84 percent.

Boston, New York and Philadelphia were the important centers for silversmithing in early America. The most famous American silversmith was Paul Revere, who is best known for his patriotic midnight ride. He was trained by his father, also named Paul Revere, who came to America from France as an silversmith apprentice. In many cases, it is hard to tell the father's work from the son's, since the two men often used the same hallmarks.

Not until American and European traders began to venture West did American Indian tribes begin to learn silversmithing. They received silver from the traders and began working it into fine ornaments and jewelry. Very little of the Indian silver work done before 1930 was marked, but today most Indian silversmiths mark their work with a personal symbol, which often also indicates their family clan. Most of their work is made from metal contain-

Left *Taking silver samples for assaying, in the London Assay office.*

Above *From 1735 to 1818, Paul Revere used either his initials or his last name, as shown in these hallmarks; each of the seven sun hallmarks belongs to a different member of the Hopi Silvercraft Guild, located on the Hopi Indian Reservation in Arizona.*

British Assay Office Silver Marks		
Prior to 1975	Standard	From 1975
🦁	Sterling silver Marked in England	🦁
🛡️	Marked in Scotland	🦁
🗽	Britannia silver	🗽

ing between 90 and 92.5 percent silver.

Unlike in the U.S., every silver object made in Great Britain must be assayed, or tested, to ensure it contains the correct amount of silver. All silver articles, whether made by hand or machine, are sent to one of the four Assay Offices in London, Birmingham, Sheffield or Edinburgh. There a small sample is scraped from each article and tested. An article that passes the assay test of purity is hallmarked with a series of stamps to identify the maker, the Assay Office, the standard of purity and the year of assay.

The practice of hallmarking goes back over 700 years in Britain. The marks are very important to connoisseurs and collectors of antique silver because they provide so much information about silver objects. Many countries in Europe belong to the International Convention, which has its own system of assay marks.

Left *The British silver marks, and* **above,** *an example of a complete hallmark.*

12. Silver coins

Ever since people started to live together in societies, they have used the barter system to exchange their surplus goods for other things that they needed. One family, for example, might trade a goat, or some chickens, in return for vegetables and grain. This barter system works well in simple societies, but becomes unmanageable when social groups grow larger and more complex. Gradually a monetary system developed in which some rare item was given an agreed value and could be used to buy goods. Many unusual things have been used for money, including shells, iron bars, salt and woven mats.

The equipment used during the Spanish conquest of South America to make coins from silver.

People soon realized that gold and silver were ideal to use as currencies because they were both rare and virtually indestructible. Small disks of precious metal, imprinted with a design, were easy to carry, difficult to forge, and were accepted almost anywhere because of the value of their precious metal content.

Early coins were literally "worth their weight in silver," and many of today's currencies were originally derived from metallic measures of weight. The Greek word *drachma*, for example, means a "handful" (of gold or silver), and the same is true of the pound, the lira and the rouble. Throughout history, there have been many famous silver coins, such as Spanish "pieces of eight" and American silver dollars.

Colonial Spanish coins, minted in Potosi in the seventeenth century.

But the ever-increasing supply of coinage throughout the world used an enormous quantity of gold and silver, and by the seventeenth century there was not enough precious metal to go around. Other metals were mixed with the gold and silver; paper money was introduced; and soon the money supply was far greater than international reserves of precious metals. In the 1970s, the United States became the last major country to eliminate all silver from its coins, though some smaller nations still use it. Today, coinage accounts for only about 8 percent of the world's total silver production.

13. Silver plating

An early French technique of electroplating, showing the article suspended in a silver solution.

Solid silver jewelry and tableware is extremely expensive, but these items can be produced much more cheaply by putting a layer of silver outside another, cheaper metal.

In 1742, a British cutler called Thomas Boulsover was working in Sheffield when he discovered the process of sandwiching a sheet of copper between thin sheets of pure silver and fusing them together. The resulting metal, called Sheffield plate, could then be worked into cutlery, tableware and candlesticks, and sold at a much lower price than articles of solid silver. These early silver-plated products followed contemporary designs and were of the highest quality. The process became obsolete in the mid-nineteenth century after the discovery of electroplating, but Sheffield plate is now highly prized, and collectors pay enormous sums for good-quality pieces.

In 1840 the process of electroplating was discovered. This produced a much thinner layer of silver, sometimes as little as one micron, or a thousandth of a millimeter thick. Because of this, the price of silver-plated articles fell even further, making it possible for many more families to afford to buy silver-plated tableware and cutlery.

Objects to be plated are made from an alloy called nickel silver. In fact, this contains no silver at all, but consists of nickel, copper and zinc. The article is suspended in a bath containing a silver solution, and an electric current is passed through the solution. The particles of silver transfer from the solution to the nickel silver article, and form a thin, even layer of pure silver on the alloy base. These articles have no hallmark, but are often marked EPNS — electroplated nickel silver.

Sometimes gold is electroplated onto articles of pure silver, to make it harder and able to withstand tarnishing. By applying different thicknesses of gold, the surface color can be made to vary from a glowing red gold to a pure and glistening white.

A Sheffield plate coffee pot, made around 1860.

31

14. Silver in photography

For centuries, scientists have known that certain silver salts and other silver compounds, called halides, darken in color when exposed to light. In the early nineteenth century, the Frenchman Joseph Nicéphore Niépce experimented with silver compounds to produce permanent images, which he called heliographs (sun-drawings). But it was his fellow-countryman Louis Daguerre who, in 1839, produced the first photograph, called a daguerrotype, using a solution of silver iodide on a copper plate. This gave a positive image of milky white on a silver background, and gave birth to the art and science of photography, which is now taken so much for granted.

A black and white negative showing the black deposits of silver salt crystals.

This enlarged photograph shows the silver halide crystals used in photographic development.

Photographic films have become far more advanced since those early days, and can now record color as well as black and white images, but they still depend on silver compounds for their sensitivity to light.

Modern photographic films are usually thin, flexible strips of transparent plastic materials, coated with a layer of emulsion, which contains silver bromide crystals suspended in a kind of gelatin. The camera shutter opens to expose these crystals to light. When treated with developing chemicals, the exposed crystals form black deposits of silver on the negative image, while unexposed crystals are dissolved by other chemicals in the fixing solution. Color films work in much the same way, but use separate layers of silver halide crystals, each with a filter for a particular color.

Photography is one of the fastest-growing industries of the century, and now uses vast quantities of silver – about one-third of the world's industrial silver consumption. But much of this is recovered and reused by burning old film and by treating used fixing solution with chemicals. Modern video cameras use magnetic tape and some new films use no silver at all, but silver will continue to play a vital role in photography for many years to come.

15. Silver in electronics

One of the most useful properties of silver is that it conducts electricity and heat better than any other metal. Because it is such a good conductor, and does not corrode, it is used in almost every type of electrical appliance. As you sit at home, you are surrounded by silver and silver alloys, in the form of switches and contacts in your television, radio, washing machine and refrigerator. Most electrical components are joined with silver solder, and the printed circuits of radios and calculators often use silver alloys as conductors.

The growth of the computer industry has created a large new market for silver, where it is used to make or coat the tiny terminals and switches in the complex and delicate circuits that make up the "brain" of a computer. Silver has proved itself to be reliable and trouble free, even in circuits that handle thousands of electronic messages every minute. Computer breakdowns are expensive in both time and money, but are rare in silver-alloy circuits.

Recently, silver has been used to make a new generation of electrical batteries, which are both smaller and more powerful than conventional batteries. Their high weight-power ratio

Right *A computer circuit board, using silver solder for the connections.*

34

makes them ideal for such special uses as hearing-aids, cameras, space satellites and submarines. Research is still continuing into the production of a silver battery that is small but powerful enough to power a car; such a battery would save valuable oil and reduce the air pollution caused by burning gasoline.

Scientists and electronics engineers are continually looking at other new energy-saving uses for silver. Silver-caesium alloy, for example, has been recently used to make powerful photoelectric cells, which convert natural sunlight into electricity. When fully developed, a single bank of these cells could possibly be used to provide enough heat and light for an entire family household.

A hot soldering iron is used to melt the silver to join two points in a circuit.

16. Industrial uses

Apart from its uses in photography and electronics, silver plays an important part in many other modern industries.

Although it does not combine easily with other substances, it is widely used in the chemical industry. That is because, in powdered form, it is a good catalyst – a substance that helps chemical changes to take place without being affected itself. As a catalyst, it is used to make certain industrial alcohols and solvents, and the ammonia compounds that are used in many modern agricultural fertilizers. Silver also plays a role in the manufacture of many synthetic fibers and washing powders.

Computer disk drives, like these awaiting export in Singapore, are coated with silver because it is a good conductor of heat and electricity.

Silver also helps the farmer and the gardener, who both use solutions of silver nitrate as fungicides to control certain plant diseases.

One of the the most exciting uses of silver is to produce rain! In recent years, large amounts of silver iodide have been used throughout the world to "seed" clouds, encouraging them to release their rain. As well as bringing rain to areas of drought, this technique can be used to release the violence of hurricanes before they do too much damage. In the right conditions,

Silver iodide can be used to encourage clouds to release their rain.

an ounce of silver iodide could produce as much as 3 million gallons of rainwater.

In the past, silver was used only for money and for making beautiful objects. But today it is seen more as an industrial metal than as a precious one, and by far the greatest part of the world's silver output is consumed by industrial manufacturers, rather than by silversmiths.

37

17. Silver in medicine

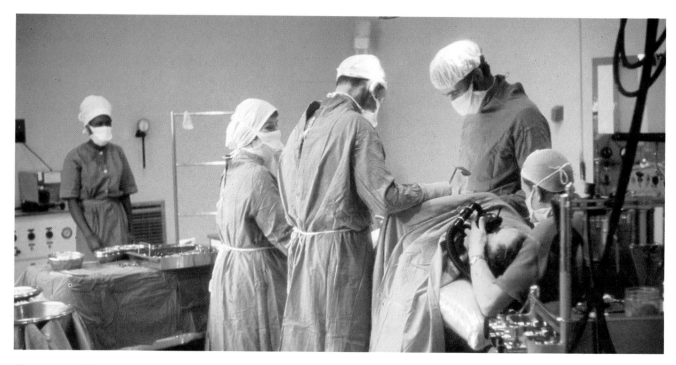

Because of its sterilizing ability, silver is widely used in surgical instruments.

Of all the many useful properties of silver, perhaps the most surprising is its ability to kill germs. This special property has been recognized and used for hundreds of years, but until recently no one understood its sterilizing ability. We now know that silver absorbs the oxygen from the air, which bacteria need to survive and breed. Many surgical instruments have traditionally been made from silver and silver alloys. The drainage tubes that often have to be inserted into the patient's body after surgery are also silver, or silver plated, to help reduce the risk of infection. Silver wire is often used to bind broken bones, and silver plate was once used to repair damaged bones and replace damaged joints.

In dentistry, silver compounds are used to fill cavities in cases of tooth decay. Dental amalgams are usually mixtures of silver, tin, and mercury, which can be easily molded to the shape of the tooth, but harden quickly to a smooth and permanent finish. The germicidal qualities of silver may also help to prevent further decay.

Because of its unique ability to absorb up to twenty times its own volume of oxygen, silver is now used for purifying water. In space, silver-based water purifiers have guaranteed astronauts a supply of bacteria-free water. The same principle is now used by campers and hikers whose only source of water may be a polluted lake or stream.

Silver compounds are used by dentists to fill cavities in teeth.

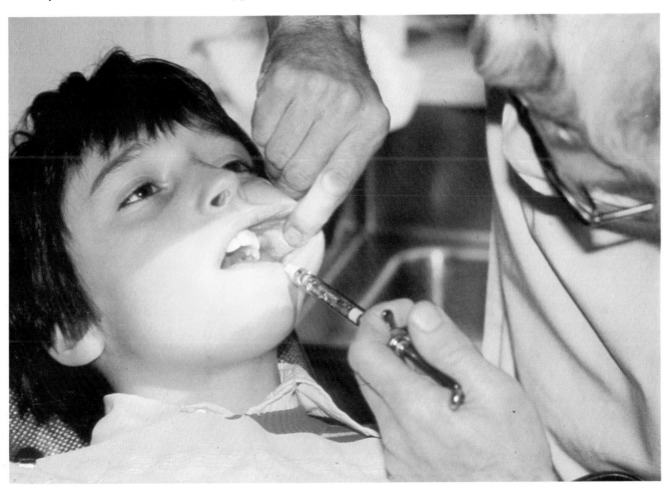

18. Buying and selling silver

Although we no longer use coins of precious metals as the basis of our money supply, gold and silver still play an important role in international trade.

Silver reserves, in the form of bars or ingots, are kept locked away in vaults, but their ownership is constantly changing, as they are bought and sold by governments and financiers on the international market. As gold has always been the treasure of kings and priests, so silver is the currency of merchants and businessmen. Today, though, much of the silver on the world's markets will be used in science, industry and the arts. The price of silver varies from country to country and from day to day. In London, the price is fixed each day by the London Spot Market Fixing system, but other countries use different systems of pricing. In 1985 the average world price for silver was $6.08 per troy ounce; this was 25 percent less than the previous year, and compared with a price of $327 per ounce for gold.

The world's main silver markets are in London, New York, Bombay and Calcutta. India has always been one of the biggest consumers of silver, to be used mainly for splendid ornaments

Right *Silver bars are stored in banks, and are bought and sold on the international market.*

The silver bullion market in Bombay, where the price of silver is fixed.

and tableware. Of the 30 billion ounces of silver estimated to have been produced throughout history, about one-eighth of that total was used in India.

In recent years, the silver market has seen some violent ups and downs, with wild fluctuations in price. That makes international trading very difficult and unpredictable, and there have been several attempts to stabilize the market.

19. The magic of silver

Silver is bound up with religion and folklore. **Left**, *an eleventh-century silver crucifix from Norway, and* **right**, *a door knocker at Durham Cathedral, England, in the shape of the crescent moon – the alchemical symbol for silver, which is supposed to ward off evil.*

Because of its beauty and its value, people have always loved silver, dreamed of it, and longed for it. Its rarity has given silver an almost magical reputation in every culture that came across it, conjuring up visions of wealth, pirates' treasure and romance.

Silver plays an important part in the fables, superstitions and folklore of many countries. It is a symbol of purity in Western and Chinese culture, and in Christianity, which uses silver chalices and candlesticks in its churches. In legends of vampires and werewolves, these beasts can only be deterred with a silver cross, or killed with a silver bullet. Just as people link gold with the sun, so silver reminds them of the pure-white light of the moon.

Poets and songwriters use silver as a favorite subject, and we have sayings like "Every cloud has a silver lining." To give someone silver is a token of love and respect, which is why medals and trophies are often made of silver. Traditionally, kings may wear crowns of gold, but princesses wear silver tiaras.

As a symbol of wealth and everlasting beauty, it carries great prestige to own and use silver articles. Perhaps that is why, in 1902, the Maharaja of Jaipur, in India, ordered an enormous pair of water jugs for his palace. Each weighing 10,408 troy oz (242.7 g), and standing 63 inches (160 cm) tall, they are the largest silver objects ever made.

For weddings and special occasions, the Indians coat sweets with edible silver paper.

Facts and Figures

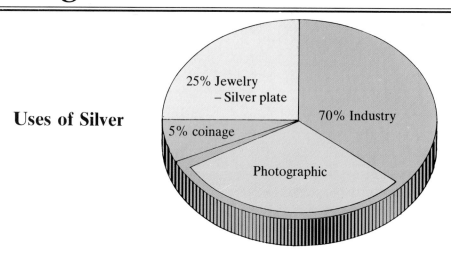

Uses of Silver

25% Jewelry
– Silver plate

5% coinage

70% Industry

Photographic

Silver Production of the Major Countries (1977-1984)
(Millions of Troy Ounces)

	1977	1978	1979	1980	1981	1982	1983	1984
U.S.S.R.	45.0	46.0	47.0	48.0	49.0	50.0	50.7	51.4
Canada	43.8	42.6	42.3	46.2	44.1	41.5	39.2	40.3
Mexico	47.0	50.6	56.1	62.2 ·	63.7	49.8	57.0	65.0
Peru	38.1	39.0	40.3	41.0	41.4	53.2	55.2	57.1
U.S.A.	38.2	41.6	46.5	48.0	46.5	40.2	43.1	47.7
Australia	25.2	24.4	25.3	24.6	24.2	29.2	33.5	33.5
Japan	9.6	9.1	9.4	9.4	9.4	9.8	9.9	9.9
Chile	6.4	6.3	5.9	5.9	6.0	12.3	14.4	13.6
Yugoslavia	4.7	4.7	4.7	4.7	4.7	3.3	3.3	3.4
Sweden	5.1	5.5	5.6	5.7	5.5	6.0	6.3	6.5
Bolivia	5.9	7.4	8.0	8.3	7.9	5.5	5.9	6.9
World Total	269.00	277.20	291.10	304.00	302.40	300.80	318.50	335.30

Features of Silver

Chemical symbol: Ag.
Atomic No.: 47
Atomic Weight: 107.873

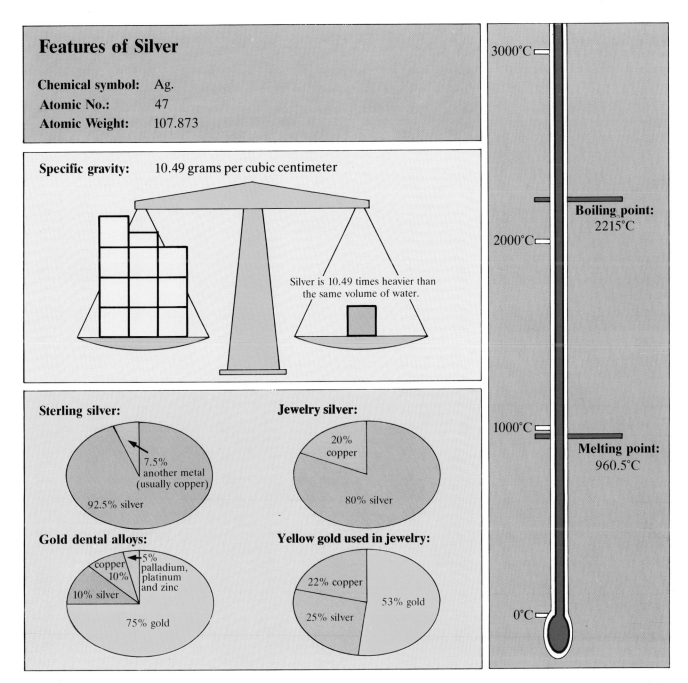

Specific gravity: 10.49 grams per cubic centimeter

Silver is 10.49 times heavier than the same volume of water.

Sterling silver:

7.5% another metal (usually copper)

92.5% silver

Jewelry silver:

20% copper

80% silver

Gold dental alloys:

copper 10%

10% silver

5% palladium, platinum and zinc

75% gold

Yellow gold used in jewelry:

22% copper

25% silver

53% gold

3000°C

Boiling point: 2215°C

2000°C

1000°C

Melting point: 960.5°C

0°C

45

Glossary

Alloy A mixture of two or more metals, created by melting them together.

Annealing Heating and cooling a piece of wrought metal to restore its malleability and keep it from cracking.

Assay To test a metal for purity.

Bullion Gold or silver in the form of a bar.

Casting The technique of making a metal object by pouring molten metal into a mold.

Catalyst A substance that helps chemical changes take place, without being changed itself.

Conductor A substance that easily transmits heat or electricity.

Currency A form of money.

Cutler Person who makes or sells cutlery.

Ductile Easy to draw out into a fine thread.

Electrolysis A process of transferring metals in solution to another substance, by passing electricity through the solution.

Engraving The art of cutting a design or pattern into the surface of an object.

Halide A chemical compound containing fluorine, chlorine, iodine or bromine.

Heirloom Precious object that is handed down through the generations of a family.

Ingot Bar of metal.

Malleable Easy to beat out into a flat sheet.

Mint Place where money is maunfactured.

Mold Hollow shape made from an original object to produce copies.

Ore Metal-bearing rock.

Porous Able to absorb other substances.

Salt A chemical substance formed by the action of an acid on a metal.

Smelt To extract metal from ore by heating it in a furnace.

Solder Alloy that melts easily to join two pieces of metal together.

Picture acknowledgments

The author and publisher would like to thank the following for allowing illustrations to be reproduced in this book: J. Allen Cash Photolibrary 11; the Bridgeman Art Library 7, 21 (bottom); Bruce Coleman 21 (top), 26; Consolidated Gold Fields 12, 19; Mary Evans Picture Library 30; Susan Griggs Agency 13; Hutchison Library 20; the Image Bank 37; Images Colour Library (Charles Walker) 42 (right); Johnson Matthey *cover*, 6, 14, 15, 18; Christine Osborne 23, 24, 36, 41, 43; Graham Rickard 25, 32, 34, 35; Science Photo Library 33; Sheffield City Museums 31; Ronald Sheridan 42 (left); South American Pictures (Tony Morrison) *frontispiece*, 8, 9 (both), 22, 28, 29, 40; Malcolm S. Walker 10, 16–17, 27.

Index